Y0-BZZ-118

ools

imagine
being blind

Linda O'Neill

The Rourke Press, Inc.
Vero Beach, Florida 32964

NOTE: Not all of the children photographed in this book are blind, but volunteered to be
photographed to help raise public awareness.

Thanks to Susan LaVenture, the executive director of NAPVI, for her support and kind
invitation to attend the very first meeting of the Florida Families of Children with Visual
Impairments. A very big thank you to all the children who visited with me that day and shared
their thoughts.

The excerpt of text from *The Vision* is reprinted with permission of Susan and Emily Townsend.

PHOTO CREDITS
© American Printing House for the Blind, Inc.: cover, page 20;
© East Coast Studios: pages 6, 9, 10, 13; © PhotoDisc: pages 15, 19, 24;
© Guide Dogs for the Blind, Inc.: page 17; © Linda O'Neill: page 23

PRODUCED & DESIGNED by East Coast Studios
eastcoaststudios.com

EDITORIAL SERVICES
Pamela Schroeder

Library of Congress Cataloging-in-Publication Data

O'Neill, Linda
   Being blind / Linda O'Neill.
     p. cm. — (Imagine...)
   Includes bibliographical references and index.
   Summary: Explains what it is like to be blind and how blind people can use Braille, guide dogs, canes,
and other aids to live independent lives.
   ISBN 1-57103-376-9
   1. Children, Blind—Juvenile literature. 2 Blindness—Juvenile literature [1. Blind. 2. Physically
handicapped.] I. Title. II. Imagine (Vero Beach, Fla.)

HV1596.3 .O54 2000
362.4'1'083—dc21

00–023923

Printed in the USA

Author's Note

This series of books is meant to enlighten and give children an awareness and sensitivity to those people who might not be just like them. We all have obstacles to overcome and challenges to meet. We need to think of the person first, not the disability. The children I interviewed for this series showed not one bit of self-pity. Their spirit and courage is admirable and inspirational.

Linda O'Neill

Table of Contents

Imagine This.................................7

Hearing 8

Touch 11

Smell.................................12

The Braille System.................................14

Guide Dogs.................................16

Games and Gadgets.................................18

Can I Help? 25

Meet Someone Special!.................................26

Glossary.................................30

Further Reading 31

Index.................................32

Imagine This

Close your eyes. Try to imagine what it would be like if you could not see. People who are blind use their other **senses** (SEN sez) to do what their eyes cannot.

When you close your eyes you can still hear your friends' voices and smell dinner cooking. You can feel soft kitten fur and taste your favorite cookie! Children who are blind can do all these things, too. They use their other senses to tell them about things around them.

Being blind does not mean you can't do things. It means you learn to do things in a different way.

Cookies taste good even if you don't see them.

7

Hearing

Your ears tell you many things. Your alarm clock tells you it is time to wake up. If you hear rain falling, you wear your raincoat to school. You know when someone comes into your room by the sound of their footsteps. Children who are blind listen very carefully to all the sounds around them. They learn to listen to the **echo** (EK oh) when they snap their fingers or clap their hands. The sound of the echo tells them if they are near an open space or a wall.

Listen to the sound echo when you snap your fingers.

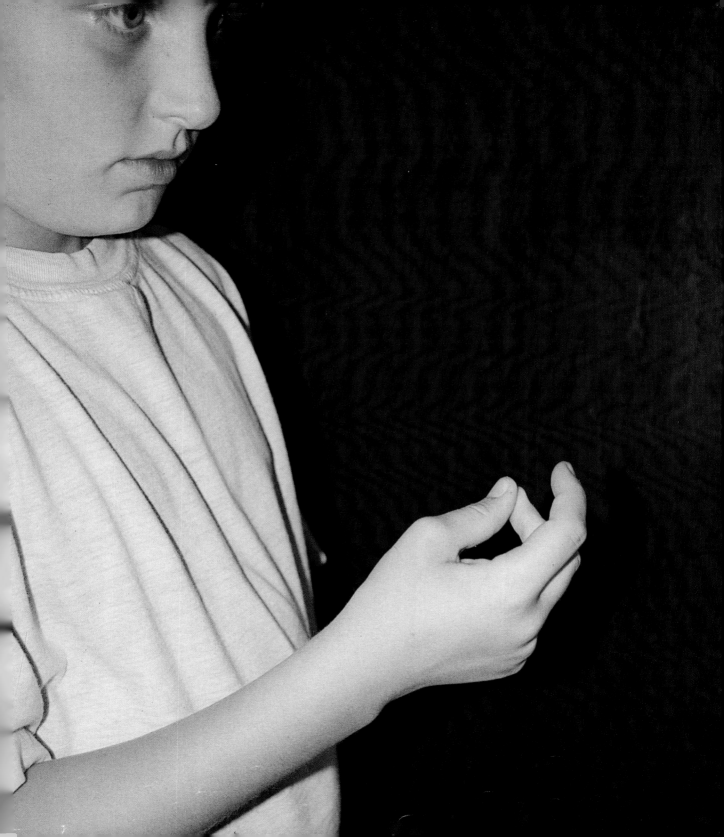

Touch

Can you tell if you have a bowl of ice cream or soup just by touching it? Ice cream is cold and soup is hot. Without looking, can you tell if you have a dime or a penny on the table? Yes, you can. Each has its own size and weight.

A bunny is soft to touch. A rock is hard. A banana feels different than an apple. The shape of a circle is not the same as the shape of a triangle.

You know all this by your sense of touch.

Can you tell which coins you have with your eyes closed?

Smell

You use your sense of smell every time you breathe. We all have smells we like and don't like. A cup of hot cocoa smells yummy, but if a skunk is near we want to hold our noses!

Everyone has a special scent. If you covered your eyes, you would still know the smell of your mom or dad. You would know the smell of a flower from the smell of peanut butter. Everything you touch has a smell. Try to see how many things you can name by just smelling them.

Smelling flowers gives your nose a treat.

The Braille System

The **Braille** (BRAYL) system for reading uses the sense of touch. It is named for Louis Braille, a blind student. He invented it in 1829. The Braille system has raised dots like tiny bumps in a "cell." Each cell stands for a letter, or word, such as "the." A person who is blind reads Braille by feeling the dots with his or her finger.

It takes a lot of practice to learn Braille. You can write Braille with a sharp tool called a **stylus** (STY lus). The stylus punches tiny holes in paper. Also, you can use a Braille typewriter. Some children learn to read Braille at five or six years old!

Reading Braille takes a lot of practice.

14

Guide Dogs

A guide dog has a very special job. Guide dogs help people who are blind get around by themselves. A guide dog learns to obey about 40 commands. They learn "turn left" and "turn right." They know when it is safe to cross the street. When they get to a curb or stairs, they stop.

Guide dog puppies start school at a year old. School takes four to six months. Then they get matched with someone who is blind. You have to be 15 or 16 years old to get a guide dog. Puppies take a lot of care. Once they get matched they go back to school— this time with their new owner. They spend many weeks learning to work together.

Guide dogs have very special jobs. They go to school, too!

Games and Gadgets

There are many tools made just for people who are blind. One is a long cane. People who are blind use the cane like an **antenna** (an TEN uh). Sweeping the cane back and forth, you can tell if something is in front of you or close to your sides.

Children who are born blind start learning this **skill** (SKIL) at a very young age. They learn how to use the cane from a **mobility** (mow BIL ah tee) teacher. This teacher shows students how to use the cane to get around easily.

This boy uses his cane to avoid bumping into anything.

ANTERIOR VIEW OF THE SKELETON

SKULL

HUMERUS

RADIUS AND ULNA

PHALANGES

FEMUR

TIBIA AND FIBULA AND PHALANGES

Braille watches help people who cannot see to tell time. The **crystal** (KRIS tahl) of the watch lifts up. You can feel the hands pointing and raised Braille dots tell you the time.

Children who are blind play some of the games that you do. There are special checkers, Scrabble, and Uno games. They play cards and many other games, too.

There are many tools, including Braille books, to help people who are blind.

Everyone can enjoy **audio** (AW dee OH) books. Your favorite stories are recorded on tape so you can listen to them. You can find many books on tape in the library.

Something new is computer software that types as you speak. You could send a letter to your Grandma without ever using a pen or pencil. Of course, you would need a computer and printer!

Tic, tac, toe *is a game everyone can play—no pencils needed.*

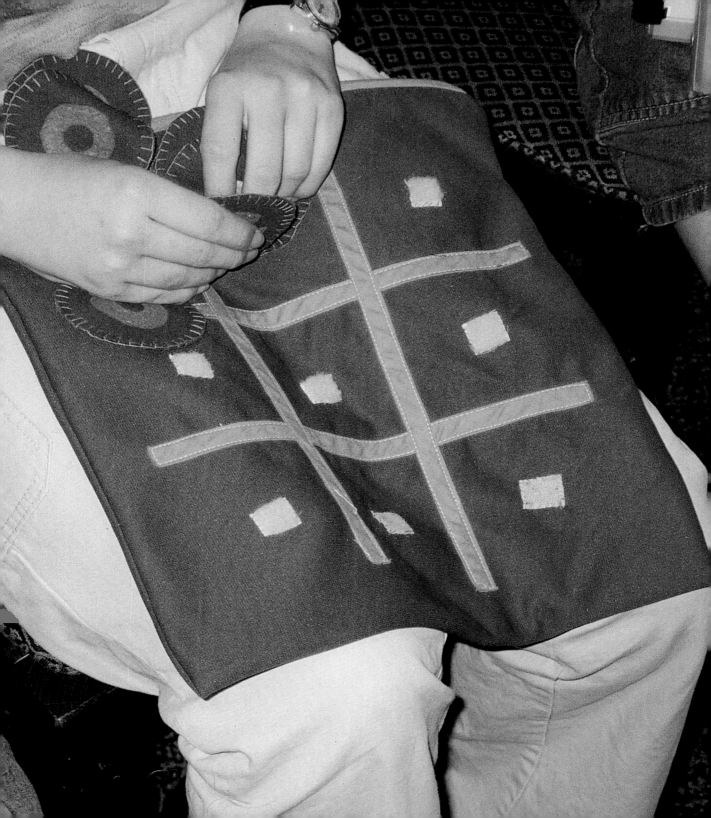

Can I Help?

People who are blind are very **independent** (IN dee PEN dent). They like to do most things for themselves. They want you to think of them as just like everyone else. Sometimes they may need your help. You should let them tell you how you can help.

Most people who are blind like to do things on their own. Sometimes a friend can be a big help.

25

Meet Someone Special!

Meet Emily

Emily is 10. Emily and her sister were born with an eye disease that makes them **visually impaired** (VIZH oo al lee im PAYRD).

Emily, is there anything special you have to do for your eye condition?
"Well, I have to wear glasses. When I was 2, I had an eye operation. I remember a stuffed elephant. My mom couldn't come in with me so she gave me this stuffed elephant. I remember people in a blue room. It was pretty scary."

Do you read Braille?
"Yes. I think it's pretty cool to be able to read both print and Braille. I am also taking mobility classes to learn caning skills."

What would you like kids to know about being visually impaired?
"That we can do things like everyone else."

Emily has written a column for *The Vision*, a newsletter for Florida Families of Children with Visual Impairment. In this column she writes:

"Most people have something that they are afraid of. My personal fear is that my eye disease will progress and my eyesight will get worse as I grow older. …What if people started treating me like a little infant? That is the last thing I want! I want to be treated like everybody else. I would like people to treat me like an average person and see me as me, and not as someone with a disability. Because if I reach into the bottom of my heart, I don't have any disabilities."

Meet Someone Special!

Meet Beth

Beth is 13 years old. She was born blind.

Beth, do you see anything at all?
   "No, being blind is like being behind a dark curtain."

Are you in school with children who are sighted?
   "Yes, I go to St. Theresa School."

Do you read Braille?
   "I started reading Braille when I was 4 years old at Early Learning Preschool."

Do you like books on tape?
   "I prefer reading with Braille. That way I can get the spelling, too."

Do you think your senses are better than sighted kids?

"My hearing is very good. When I play my radio, it's so low no one else can hear it. My fingers are very sensitive, too."

How do you find your way around when you go into a new place?

"When going into a new room, I feel everything I can and then I remember where things are."

What do you like to do with your friends?

"My friend Angelica and I like to talk on the phone and watch movies together. Angelica is sighted so she tells me what is happening."

What would you like to do when you are older?

"I would like a singing job. I'd like to tour with the Backstreet Boys."

What would you like other kids to know about being blind?

"Today's focus is all on looks and this is very unfriendly to vision impaired or blind people."

Glossary

antenna (an TEN uh) — a movable sensor

audio (AW dee OH) — having to do with sound

Braille (BRAYL) — a system of reading and writing for the blind

crystal (KRIS tahl) — the clear cover over the face of a watch

echo (EK oh) — a repeating of sound; the sound bounces off something and comes back to you

independent (IN dee PEN dent) — not relying on others to assist you

mobility (mow BIL ah tee) — ability to move around

senses (SEN sez) — how people and animals learn about the world around them: sight, hearing, taste, touch, smell

skill (SKIL) — an ability to do something well

stylus (STY lus) — a pen-shaped tool with a sharp point

visually impaired (VIZH oo al lee im PAYRD) — damaged eyesight

Further Reading

Arnold, Caroline. *A Guide Dog Puppy Grows Up*. Harcourt Brace & Co, 1991

Carter, Alden R. *Seeing Things My Way*. Albert Whitman & Co. 1998

Landau, Elaine. *Blindness: Understanding Illness*. Twenty First Century Books, 1995

Patten, J. *Working Dogs*. Rourke Publishing Group, 1996

Visit these Websites
National Federation for the Blind
www.nfb.org

Southeastern Guide Dogs
www.guidedogs.org

Guide Dogs for the Blind, Inc.
www.guidedogs.com

American Printing House for the Blind, Inc.
www.aph.org

Index

audio books   22

Braille   14, 21, 26, 28

cane   18

cell   14

echo   8

games   21, 22

guide dog   16

mobility teacher   18

puppies   16

school   16

senses   7

tools   18